T0368469

TO: _____

I hope you enjoyed this book from ear to tail! My prayer for you is _____

_____

_____

_____

_____

Yours truly,

_____

AuthorHouse™
1663 Liberty Drive
Bloomington, IN 47403
www.authorhouse.com
Phone: 1 (800) 839-8640

NIV

Scripture quotations marked NIV are taken from the Holy Bible, New International Version®. NIV®. Copyright © 1973,
1978, 1984 by International Bible Society. Used by permission of Zondervan. All rights reserved. [Biblica]

NLT

Scripture quotations marked NLT are taken from the Holy Bible, New Living Translation, copyright © 1996, 2004, 2007.
Used by permission of Tyndale House Publishers, Inc. Carol Stream, Illinois 60188. All rights reserved. Website

NRSV

Scripture quotations marked NRSV are taken from the New

Published by AuthorHouse 09/21/2015

ISBN: 978-1-5049-4988-0 (sc)
ISBN: 978-1-5049-4989-7 (e)

Library of Congress Control Number: 2015915229

Print information available on the last page.

authorHOUSE®

Dog Spelled Backwards

Arlette Martin

There is something about having a pet that is comforting and peaceful, which is why I decided to write this book and share our family pet, Minnie Mouse, with you. She's just so adorable that you cannot help but love her.

"Whoever does not love does not know God, because God is love." 1 John 4:8 (NIV)

This is Minnie Mouse (aka Mouse) as a pup.

Before I start our story about Mouse, I think it is only fitting to share our story about K.C. and C.C. If it were not for them, the Mouse would not be with us today.

K.C., named after Aunt Kris and Aunt Carrie, lived with us for approximately sixteen years. I say *approximately* because the family still to this day debates about when she was born. K.C., having been a mother of two litters, had no hard feelings at the young age of ten when our human baby came along. K.C. let the baby fit right in.

"Children are a gift from the lord; they are a reward from him." Psalm 127:3 (NLT)

K.C.

One thing we can say is that K.C. was an old pup upon her passing on December 16, 2000.

"For we believe that Jesus died and rose again, and so we believe that God will bring with Jesus those who have fallen asleep in him." 1 Thessalonians 4:14 (NIV)

K.C. passed when our daughter was six years old. We decided we should wait to get another dog until our daughter was old enough to help take care of a pet. Is that not the way all parents do this, to avoid the jolt of taking care of a puppy?

"But if we hope for what we do not yet have, we wait for it patiently." Romans 8:25 (NIV)

And so we waited and waited until our daughter was ten years old. Then along came C.C., a Bernese mountain dog named after the Chicago Cubs; born into a Cubs family, it was only fitting. C.C. brought about a lot of change for us. K.C. had always been an outside dog, and C.C. was going to be an inside dog. God sent us a house dog that would change us all forever. C.C. made the family complete, so to speak. She gave our daughter Ms. Alika a sister and a friend.

God said to Moses, "I am who I am." This is what you are to say to the Israelites: 'I am has sent me to you.'" Exodus 3:14 (NIV)

"A friend loves at all times and a brother is born for a time of adversity." Proverbs 17:17 (NIV)

"And Jonathan made a covenant with David because he loved him as himself." 1 Samuel 18:3 (NIV)

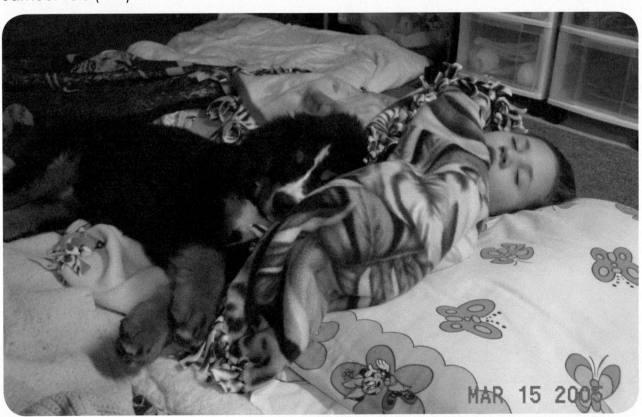

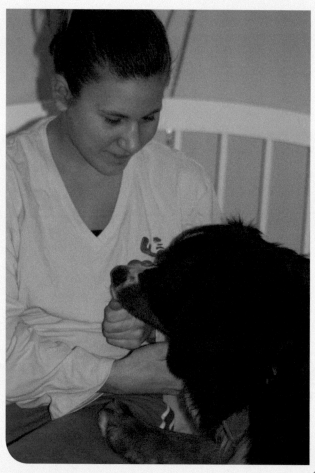

Play Hard

WORK HARD

"The student is not above the teacher, but everyone who is fully trained will be like their teacher." Luke 6:40 (NIV)

Puppy School

"And Jonathan made a covenant with David because he loved him as himself." 1 Samuel 18:3 (NIV)

JUN 4 2005

"All kinds of animals, birds, reptiles, and sea creatures are being tamed and have been tamed by mankind." James 3:7 (NIV)

I had always thought K.C. was a calm, even-tempered dog, and C.C. was just as docile. Dressing up the puppy dog ranks up there as a little girl's all-time favorite thing to do.

 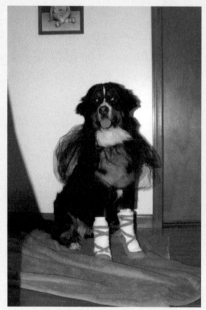 

"Your beauty should not come from outward adornment, such as elaborate hairstyles and wearing of gold jewelry or fine clothes. Rather, it should be that of your inner self, the unfading beauty of a gentle and quiet spirit, which is of great worth in God's sight." 1 Peter 3:3–4 (NIV)

"Give thanks to the God of heaven. His love endures forever." Psalm 136:26 (NIV)
I give thanks to the Lord for giving us such a precious gift: C.C.

JUL 17 2005

MAR 19 2006

"But it is you, a man like myself, my companion, my close friend, with whom I once enjoyed sweet fellowship at the house of god, as we walked about among the worshipers." Psalm 55:13–14 (NIV)

C.C. had a couple of gastric volvulus (bloat) episodes, but none was life-threatening. C.C. sadly passed away at the young age of two and a half on May 21, 2007 from another episode of bloat. It still saddens me to this day. She was so young and sweet. C.C.'s death was a tragedy for us all. C.C. was a loving indoor dog. She changed the atmosphere of the house. C.C. was well loved and cared for. Her death didn't make sense. I believe all dogs go to heaven. It just so happens that God was calling C.C. to be an angel pup.

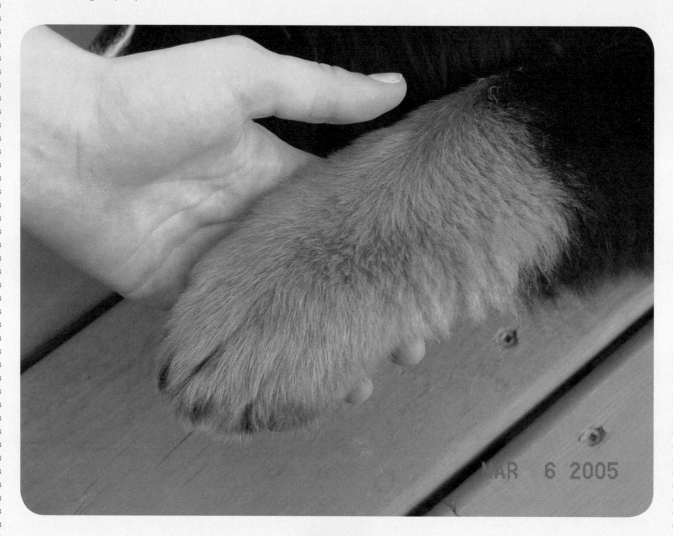

MAR 6 2005

Forever Friends!

"Look on me and answer, Lord my God. Give light to my eyes, or I will sleep in death."
Psalm 13:3 (NIV)

"Now then, stand and see this great thing the LORD is about to do before your eyes!" 1 Samuel 12:16 (NIV)

C.C.'s death was devastating, and the so-called silence was unbearable. I say "so-called" because even though C.C. was no longer in the house with us, her spirit was. In the basement, I could still hear her nails hitting the wood floor above. I could still hear her tail hitting the wall as she would wait at the kitchen door for us to come home. The silence made us miss her more.

And so the story begins of a Mouse in the house.

My niece Emily knew that I had wanted an Afghan hound, and so the Internet search was on. She found us a pup in Chicago. Before we had even met the dog, we had picked out the name Minnie Mouse for our new Afghan puppy. Once we made our two-hour trip to Chicago, we found out Minnie Mouse's dad was named Pinocchio! How could we have unknowingly picked such a perfect name?

Pictured above: Mouse's dad

Picture below: Mouse's ma

"And in the fire was what looked like four living creatures. In appearance their form was human." Ezekiel 1:5 (NIV)

Today, Mouse is the young age of eight. It seems as though she has been with us all our lives, though. It amazes me how humanlike she is to the family.

Mouse sitting humanlike

Is it okay to let the baby watch TV?

Mouse is the baby of the family. She sleeps like a baby, too!

"I will refresh the weary and satisfy the faint. At this I awoke and looked around. My sleep had been pleasant to me." Jeremiah 31:25–26 (NIV)

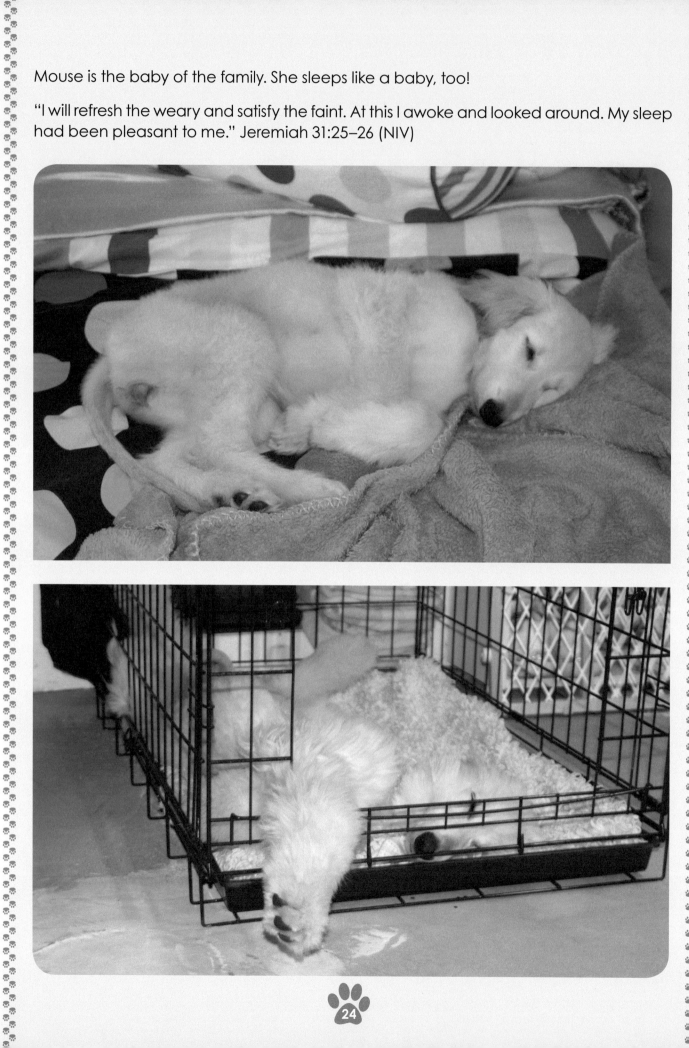

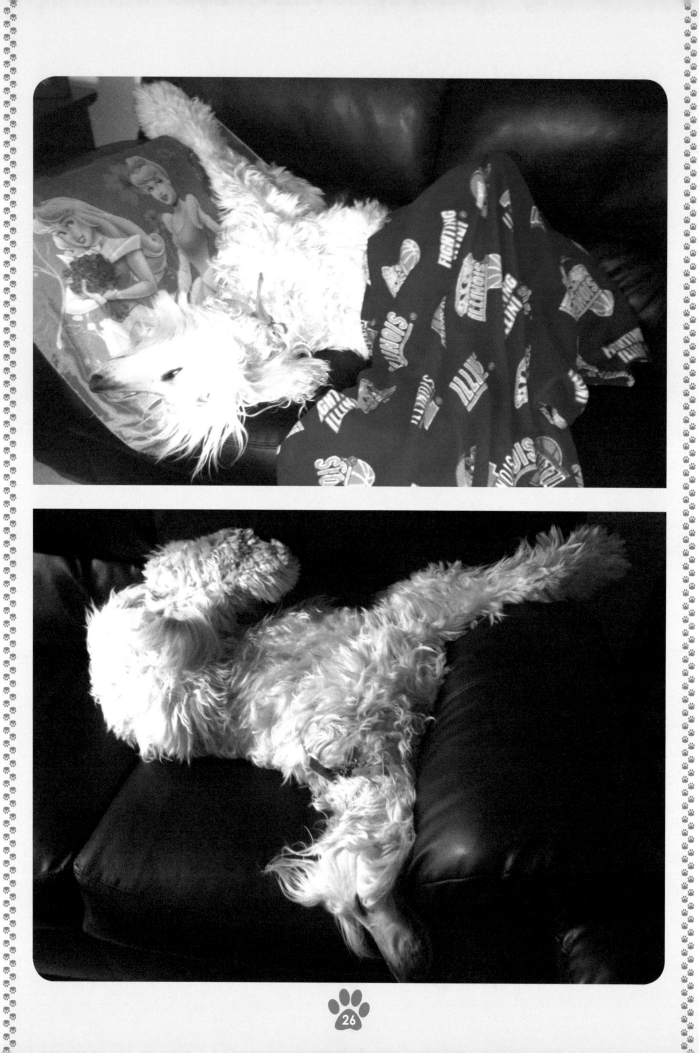

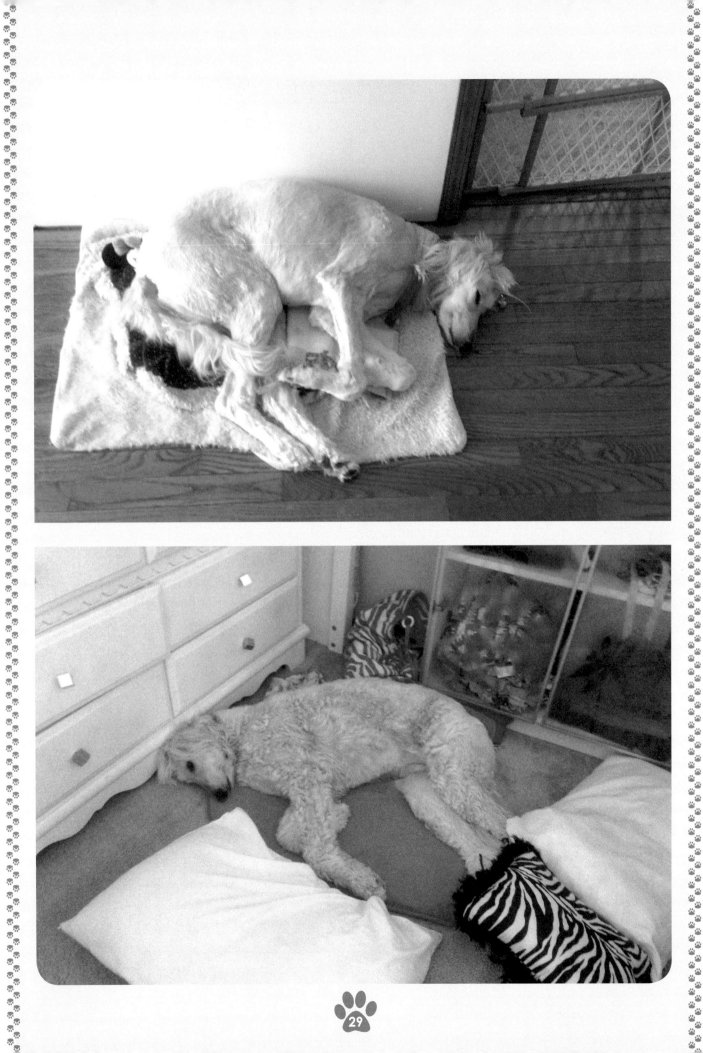

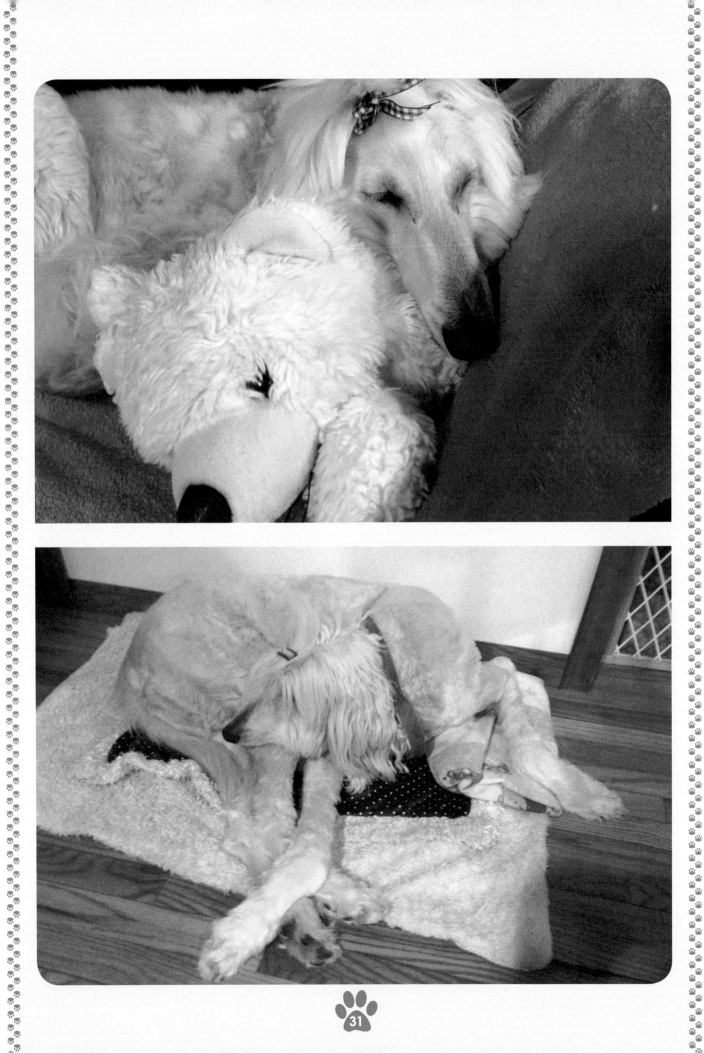

Mouse sleeps so peacefully!

"Whoever dwells in the shelter of the Most High will rest in the shadow of the Almighty. I will say of the Lord, 'He is my refuge and fortress, my God, in whom I trust.'" Psalm 91:1–2 (NIV)

Mouse patiently waits for her human sister to awaken after eye surgery.

"See, I am sending an angel ahead of you to guard you along the way and to bring you to the place I have prepared." Exodus 23:20 (NIV)

Do not let the sleeping Mouse fool you. She can be a mischievous Mouse!

Mouse's all-time favorite activity is tipping her toys over! It's a nightly event!

Here she is caught rooting through her human sister's cheer bag.

Then she was caught stealing a sandwich out of the lunch bag.

Instead of reading the camera guide, she decided to eat it. Maybe that's because I take too many pictures of her! A whole new perspective on digesting information.

"The righteous person may have many troubles, but the lord delivers him from them all." Psalm 34:19 (NIV)

Although Mouse may be a bit of a troublemaker, she truly brings happiness to all!

"Blessed are those whose help is the God of Jacob, whose hope is in the Lord their God." Psalm 146:5 (NIV)

It is true: the more we walk with God, the happier we become. How fitting that a daily walk with the Mouse brings peace and happiness to me.

Mouse always has a smile.

"He will yet fill your mouth with laughter and your lips with shouts of joy." Job 8:21 (NIV)

Whether it is hide-and-seek, playing in the snow, or playing dress-up, Mouse is always a good sport.

"Create in me a pure heart, O God, and renew a steadfast spirit within me." Psalm 51:10 (NIV)

I hope you will find joy in K.C., C.C., and the Mouse's story . If not in them, maybe you'll find hope and laughter in someone or something, like our pups have for us. I have so many pictures of Mouse that it is truly difficult to choose. I know I cannot share them all. My hope is that you see the love and joy she has brought us in the pictures I have shared. I hope she makes you smile like she makes us smile. Someday when she's gone, we will still have the memories of her friendship, a simple reminder of peace and happiness!

I truly miss K.C. and C.C., but there is something to be said about a Mouse in the house. I once read that the Afghan hound is said to be called the "dog of Noah's ark." I'm reminded that *dog* spelled backwards is "God." Mouse is not God, but God is in her, and she has helped me connect to Him. I look at her, and I see the unconditional love she gives us over and over again. "For God so loved the world he sent His only son to die for us." God loves us. Mouse loves us. Through their light, I see we need to love one another.

My prayer for you is that you find your "God spelled backwards" and embrace it!

"May the God of hope fill you with all joy and peace as you trust in him, so that you may overflow with hope by the power of the Holy Spirit." Romans 15:13 (NIV)

God bless!

Printed in the United States
By Bookmasters